Meals ..., Mothers Taught Me

Four generations of kitchen know-how in one volume

As created, recreated, remembered and shared

By Diana Phillips

First collected for my grandson

Sam Cohen

on his leaving home and fending and cooking for himself

And subsequently coveted, copied and treasured by the rest of the family

ISBN 978-1482390148

First published in hardback by imprint illyria 2009

This paperback edition published by imprint illyria 2013
Distributed through Create Space

© Diana Phillips 2009, 2013

www.imprintillyria.com

Meals My Mothers Taught Me

by

Diana Phillips

With fond memories and many grateful thanks to my mothers and grandmother and family and friends whose advice, wisdom, skill and knowledge are so generously shared in these pages.

Once upon a Friday Night ...

Di Phillips was blessed with two wonderful mothers.

Her own mother was Mummy, Hetty Passman, to be known to generations to come as Nana Passman. Hetty had a heart of gold and just as magical a Midas touch in both the haimishe and contemporary kitchen and blessed with the knowledge and know how of her own mother "Booba" Rosenberg.

When Di married Ronald Phillips she gained a second mother. Eva Phillips, née Colman, who had long been Di's Auntie Eva, was now to become Mum, Queen of the Friday night shabbos meal.

Through more than half a century the recipes of her mothers and grandmothers continued to grace Di's table, ever augmented with her own creations and those of her friends and wider family, from sister Janet to lifelong chums. Her children, Laurence and Hélène, grew up with these favourite meals. As Hélène's four sons, Sam, Joe, Benjy and Zak, came to take control of the family meals (and especially when Sam left home) Di, by now not only Mummy to her own children, but also Bibby to her grandsons, began to collect the recipes she knew by heart and soul to pass down the secrets of generations past to the generations of the future.

Contents

Soups & Starters

Page 7

Main Courses

Page 33

Desserts

Page 73

Index

Page 96

Soups & Starters

Booba's
BORSHT

> 4lb new baby beetroots
> 1 tablespoon pearl barley
> sugar/sweetener, to taste
> acetic acid, to taste
> boiling water

Wash, peel and slice the beets. Place the barley under an upturned saucer on the base of a large saucepan.

Spread the sliced beets on top carefully. Cover with boiling water, then add sugar/sweetener and acetic acid to taste.

Always use acetic acid sparingly and never breathe in their fumes. Alternatively lemon juice or vinegar can be used.

Cover with a lid and leave a small opening for the steam to escape, and cook gently over a very low heat until the beets are soft. If you cook this on too high a temperature, a larger quantity of the liquid will evaporate.

Chill and remove the beets carefully - without disturbing the upturned saucer over the barley.

Then, strain the liquid and the starch from the barley will help to give the Borsht more body.

This freezes excellently. It may be served either hot or cold from the fridge.

If served hot, you can thicken it even more by taking an egg yolk and mixing it well with a small amount of the liquid once it is hot and then adding it to the rest of the soup. Hot, it is delicious served with a scoop of freshly mashed potato and (with a milk meal) a swirl of sour cream.

If served cold, just add the sour cream and maybe some chopped chives for garnish.

Discarded beets are ideal for a salad dish with finely chopped spring onions.

Booba (front right) knew how to put a smile and a glow on her family's faces

CHICKEN SOUP
(aka Jewish Penicillin)

The most economical and tasty recipe is followed using either chicken frames (raw carcases) or merely plenty of giblets. This way, the soup goes to a complete jelly and is a perfect version of the 'hoiste fenster's' consomme!

2-3 packets chicken frames
(or 6-8 sets of giblets)
3 large carrots
3 sticks celery
3 large leeks
1 parsnip (optional)
1 large tomato
salt/pepper

If using frames, scald them with boiling water first and make sure they are free from any blood etc.

Place in a large saucepan, cover with water and bring to the boil, skimming till the water is clear.

If using giblets, treat in the same way, after removing the chicken livers and setting aside. These livers can be used for a delicious risotto or added to chopped liver or (even better yet) saved for my Booba's special recipe *Chicken Livers with Egg*, (see page 34).

Once the water is clear, add the vegetables and seasoning and cook very slowly till giblets are soft and falling apart.

Strain the soup through a mesh sieve to ensure that there are no small bones left.

The chicken may then be removed from the bones and used in various dishes. Very economical, you can make several different meals from the bits!

Should you need extra quantities but not have enough chicken you can always add a chicken stock cube.

And to complete the full experience, don't forget the *kneidlach* (turn the page).

KNEIDLACH
(matzo balls)

> 2 eggs
> 2 tablespoons soft vegetable (or chicken) fat
> 2 cups warm water
> medium/fine matzo meal (mixed)
> Salt and pepper

Beat eggs with salt and pepper, add soft fat and water, gradually add fine and medium meal till slightly firm.

Roll into balls and arrange on large tray and fridge for while till cold.

Add balls to boiling stock and cook for aproximately 10 minutes.

Remove carefully, lay the balls evenly on tray and freeze.

> Once frozen they may be bagged and stored.

CHOPPED EGGS & ONIONS

---

4 hardboiled eggs
bunch spring onions
salt and pepper
chopped parsley
soft margarine
(or "light touch" – note non parve)

Grate or "mouli" the eggs, chop the onions and parsley finely.

Mix all together, add seasoning, and gradually blend together with the fat.

Chill and serve, with crackers, rye bread or salad as a starter.

This mixture can also be used in canapés or bridge rolls or even as a delicious sandwich filling for light snacks and picnics.

FRESH PEA & MINT SOUP

450grams/1lb fresh or frozen peas
2 leeks chopped
1-2 tablespoons freshly chopped mint
1pint (approx) pareve chicken stock
1 tablespoon plain flour
¾ pint milk (or soya, if meat dish to follow)
knob of soft margarine or lite oil
1 stick celery sliced thinly
freshly ground black pepper
fresh mint sprigs for garnish.

In large microwave bowl, place the fat, leeks, celery peas and mint. Then, cover and microwave for approximately 6 minutes. Check and stir halfway.

Remove from microwave and add the stock and seasoning, cover and cook for a further 5 minutes.

In separate bowl, blend the flour with the milk/soya milk until it is smooth. Then, gradually add to the soup.

Remove from the microwave and leave to cool.

Once cooled, blend, and return to microwave for a further 5 minutes. Again, check and stir halfway.

Leave in fridge before serving.

Add a swirl of pouring cream: either dairy or soya will work equally well. Top off with sprig of mint.

LEEK, LENTIL & ORANGE SOUP

---

3 leeks
juice of 1 orange, squeezed
some of the orange rind, finely shredded.
6-8 oz red lentils
1 stick celery
small carrot chopped finely or grated.
fresh herbs (ie thyme, or mixed Italian)
2 pints pareve chicken stock (approx)
freshly ground black pepper
2 oz soft margarine or lite oil

Wash lentils, then place them in a large microwave bowl with sliced leeks, celery, carrot.

Cover and cook in the microwave for approximately 2 minutes.

Remove from the microwave and immediately stir the ingredients vigorously in order to prevent the lentils from sticking together.

Add the stock and the remaining ingredients.

Replace in the microwave, cover and cook for approximately 16 minutes, or until the lentils have broken down and are soft.

Leave to cool. Blend, and then, if necessary, add more fresh orange juice to taste.

Serve, garnished with chopped fresh parsley and finely shredded orange peel.

This soup freezes very well. Like all blended soups, it will require a quick re-blend once defrosted as soups tend to separate and appear fibrous.

Nana Passman's
CHOPPED LIVER

> 3 packs of chicken livers (koshered)
> 3 large onions
> simulated chicken fat
> (cholesterol free – counteracts the cholesterol in the livers, I wish!!)
> salt and pepper
> sash of cinnamon

Wash and dry the livers. Then, slice the onions.

In a large frying pan, already greased with the simulated chicken fat, gently sauté the onions, seasoning well, until they appear soft and transparent.

Remove the onions from the pan; now, add the livers and sauté quickly, turning all the time till thoroughly cooked.

Mince all the ingredients together. Add more seasoning to taste and just a small dash of cinnamon.

If necessary add more fat, or if freezing leave

adding extra fat till the mixture has defrosted and then add if required.
You can also add a minced hardboiled egg at this stage;

I, personally, do not add the egg until I am ready to serve this dish as frozen hard-boiled eggs can become rubbery in texture.

This dish freezes particularly well.

Nana brought the Rosenberg women's recipes to the Passman family when she (Hetty) married Papa (Sid).

Nana Phillips'
CARROT TZIMMES

3lb top rib, stewing meat, cut into chunks
2-3 lb carrots, sliced
2-3 potatoes, cut into chunks
flour
vegetable fat
(parve cooking margerine or simulated chicken schmaltz)
sugar/sweetener

Put the meat into large saucepan, cover with water. Bring to boil and skim, then add the carrots, potatoes, a dash of salt and pepper, and the sweetener or sugar.

Cover and cook slowly over a low heat.

About an hour before serving, prepare the dumplings - rub some vegetable fat (see above) into the flour with a little seasoning.

Make into a more pliable dough by gradually adding a little water.

Then, drop small spoonfuls into the saucepan and

they will cook in about 10-15 minutes.

Serve straight away.
This is another 'all-in-one' haimishe meal

Again brought over by our grandparents from Eastern Europe.

A cheap, peasant dish but full of flavour and nutrients: ideal on a cold winter evening.

Nana Phillips (Eva) knew the way to Papa's (Harry's) heart and to the hearts of the family was through good old fashioned bullebuste home cooking.

Hanne's
BUTTERNUT SQUASH & GINGER SOUP

2lb butternut squash (approx)
1 medium onion, chopped
1½ tablespoons coarsely chopped fresh ginger
2 cloves garlic, chopped
2 oz margarine (*Light Touch is non parve*)
2 pints stock (pareve chicken)
2 teaspoons fresh lime juice
black pepper, salt

Slice and peel the squash, making sure to remove the seeds.

Sauté the onions, ginger and garlic until soft (covered). The add the squash and stock, re-cover and bring to boil, then simmer for around 20 minutes or until squash is soft.

Cool, blend and add seasoning if necessary.

Can be frozen, but like all blended soups will need lightly re-blending as it becomes fibrous after freezing.

Serve with thin slices of lime zest peelings.

CAPONATA
EGGPLANT-APPETISER

½ cup olive oil
1 large aubergine, washed dried and cubed
1 cup diced celery
2 cups chopped onion
1 clove garlic, chopped
2 cups tomato sauce
¼ cup red wine vinegar
1 tablespoon honey
2 tablespoons drained chopped capers
⅔ cup drained chopped stuffed olives
freshly ground black pepper & salt

Heat oil, sauté the aubergine till tender, remove from the pan, add celery, onion and garlic and sauté till tender, stir in tomato sauce and cooked aubergine, cover and simmer for aproximately 15 minutes or until the mixture is thick and well coked. Stir occasionally, taste and add seasonings accordingly to taste.

Cool, then chill covered with Cling film for at least 4 hours, preferably overnight. Can be kept for several days in the fridge or may also be frozen.

Serve with rounds of toast, crusty bread, large croutons or crackers. Can also be used with crudités. Serves approximately 8.

WATERCRESS & PEA SOUP

> 1½ litres stock (pareve chicken is ideal)
> 6 spring onions
> 4 cloves garlic
> 450 grams peas (frozen)
> watercress or other green veg, (eg: rocket, spinach etc.)
> 150ml cream (soya is fine and not so rich)

Chop the spring onions, and the garlic then add to the stock in a saucepan. Season, cover and bring to boil until the onions begin to appear glassy.

Next, add the green leaves and peas and cook for a few minutes until the peas are soft.

Remove the saucepan from the heat, and now stir in the cream.

Blend and serve.

Garnish with fresh herb leaves or a sprig of mint from the garden.

GAZPACHO

2 cartons of tomato juice *(Sainsbury's is best)*
2 cloves garlic, chopped finely
2 large onions (sweet), chopped finely
2 red peppers, chopped
1 green pepper, chopped
2 cucumbers, chopped
sprinkle of sugar/sweetener to taste
home made vinaigrette to taste

Pour the tomato juice into large bowl.

Next chop all vegetables and add to juice. The vegetables should be chopped finely, but still large enough to retain a good crunch.

Stir the vegetables and juice well, Season to taste and add some home made vinaigrette and sweetener to taste.

Chill and serve with home made croutons.

Very refreshing for a balmy summer evening when dining 'al fresco'.

Laurence's
FRENCH ONION SOUP

4-6 large onions
(Spanish or – better still - sweet Cevennes)
1 litre or more pareve or chicken stock
30g approx butter – or healthier equivalent thereof
Marmite
pepper to taste
croutons
grated gruyere cheese

First slice the onions, quite finely. Hold a metal teaspoon between your teeth to avoid tears.

In a large saucepan, gently melt the butter before adding the onions.

Stir occasionally until they become transparent.

Then pour in the stock (either from chicken carcasses or giblets, or a vegetable or pareve stock cube/powder) and bring to the boil.

Add a generous spoonful of Marmite.

A good tip is to save "empty" Marmite jars and swirl around with the stock to remove the last traces of Marmite from the jar.

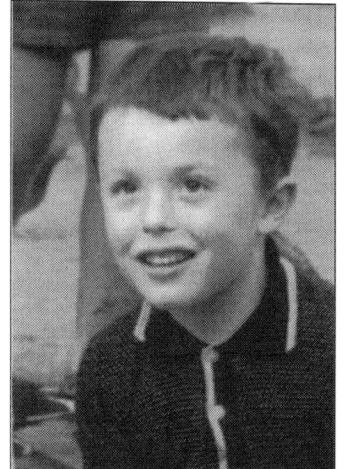

Leave to simmer on a low heat for as long as you like, before serving, much later in the day.

Top up with hot water or stock as you wish. Add a twist or two of black pepper

Ladle a generous helping into a deep soup bowl, then place a toasted crouton (or few) atop the onions and sprinkle lavishly with grated gruyere cheese.

Spanish onions provide a strong hearty flavour, whilst Cevennes or Lezignan sweet onions create a subtle light and aromatic alternative.

SMOKED MACKEREL PATE

> packet of smoked mackerel fillets
> (the peppered variety is excellent)
> mayonnaise
> horseradish sauce,
> lemon juice
> balsamic vinegar
> chopped fresh parsley
> seasonings
> chopped capers (optional)

Skin the fillets, and flake the fish into bowl, add a tablespoon of mayonnaise, and a similar amount of horseradish sauce.

A squeeze of lemon juice, small amount of balsamic vinegar, chopped parsley.

Blend all ingredients together with a fork mixing well till fairly smooth, if using a blender it becomes more pureed.

Personally, I prefer the mixture to be roughly blended by hand to create the coarser texture of a traditional Normandy *rillettes*" pate.

The various seasonings will have to be adjusted according to personal taste. You may prefer more mayonnaise, less horseradish etc.

Once it is blended to your taste, line a fish mould or any shape mould with cling film.

Press in the mixture, cover with cling film and place in fridge till ready to eat.

It can then be turned out onto serving plate and garnished accordingly.

This dish may be served as a starter, even a sandwich or jacket potato filling or simply as a picnic or lunchtime dip. It is particularly good when served with crisp chicory or celery.

SWEET & SOUR CABBAGE BORSHT
(Nanas Passman and Phillips' recipe)

> large white Dutch cabbage, finely shredded
> 2-3 lb top rib or stewing meat, cut into chunks.
> 2-3 large potatoes, cut into chunks
> sultanas/raisins
> water
> sugar/sweetener
> acetic acid/brown vinegar/lemon juice.

Place the meat in a large saucepan, cover with water, bring to the boil and them remove any scum or froth. If necessary, remove the meat and then start again once the water is clear. Then, add the shredded cabbage and potatoes, add sweet and sour seasoning to taste. Cover the saucepan, leaving small gap for the steam to escape, and cook slowly for several hours on the lowest temperature.

After about 2 hours add the raisins/sultanas.

> Serve as an 'all in one' dish. This is always nicer the following day

TOMATO SOUP WITH RICE & BASIL

1oz Light Touch *(non parve)*, olive oil, butter, or margarine
(whichever preferred)
1 large onion, chopped
40 grams (1½ oz) plain flour
2 tablespoons tomato puree
750 gms (1 ½ lb) ripe tomatoes cut into quarters
¼ teaspoon celery salt
1 teaspoon caster sugar /Splenda
1 teaspoon chopped fresh basil
salt and pepper
½ pt milk or soya substitute
¾ pt pareve chicken stock
4 teaspoons cooked rice
2 teaspoons single cream or soya cream

Pace fat in large bowl, soften in either microwave or on top of cooker. Stir in flour tomato puree, tomatoes, celery, salt sugar basil salt and pepper. Add stock cover and cook for 10 minutes, stirring halfway.

Allow to cool slightly, blend till smooth. Sieve if necessary. Stir in cooked rice.

Serve and garnish with fresh basil leaves and a swirl of cream.

TOMATO SOUP WITH GIN

> 1-2 lb ripe tomatoes, skinned
> 2 - 3 leeks, chopped
> 1 oz margarine
> 2 tablespoons red lentils
> tomato puree
> celery
> sugar/salt/pepper, to taste
> chicken stock (parve)
> gin, to taste

Sweat the lentils, leeks, celery in microwave for approximately 2-3 minutes. Add the tomatoes, puree and rest of ingredients.

Cover and microwave for approximately 15 minutes or until the lentils are completely soft.

Stir, taste, cool and blend. Once blended, season again to taste and check if more gin is needed.

Garnish with swirl of soured cream, crème fraiche or whatever.

> Stéphane serves this soup with a spoonful of blue cheese at the bottom of the bowl (typically *St Agur*). He also uses continental *genièvre* gin for a stronger flavour of juniper.

Main Courses

Booba's
CHICKEN LIVER & EGG BAKE

> 2 packets chicken livers
> 4 eggs, beaten
> 4 shallots
> lite oil (or *schmaltz*)
> salt and pepper
> 2 medium potatoes, sliced

Peel and slice the potatoes and boil them gently till almost soft.

Wash the livers, pat dry with kitchen paper, season well.

Chop the shallots and sweat them lightly in a non-stick pan using a very small amount of lite oil or better still some vegetable 'chicken fat' *schmaltz* (cholesterol free!).

Grease an oven dish, then spread the shallots on the bottom. Now, add the seasoned chicken livers, sliced potatoes and pour the seasoned beaten egg mixture over and bake slowly in the oven till the egg and livers are cooked.

Ensure that the livers are cooked through. This dish can be prepared at the last minute, just before eating.

Apparently, this was my mother's favourite supper dish when she would return home after performing in a concert (Nana is pictured, with her violin, 2nd from left, middle row). My Booba felt it was a 'nourishing and not too heavy meal' to go to bed with!!

BAKED MEATLOAF

---

2 lb minced meat
(beef or turkey/chicken mince)
shallots
jar of tomato and mushroom pasta sauce
1 glove of garlic, grated or chopped finely
1 glass of red wine,
(if using poultry, it is best to marinade the meat in red wine for about half an hour before preparing this dish)
salt and pepper
fresh herbs, chopped
3 tomatoes, chopped or sliced
sliced mushrooms (optional)

Sauté the finely chopped shallots and garlic gently. Mix the mince well with the sauce and all the other ingredients.

Line two non-stick loaf tins with cake liners, and press the mixture into the tins. Place both tins on a baking tray and bake in medium oven for approximately half an hour.

Once the meat has begun to set in the tins and feels fairly firm to the touch, turn out the loaves from the tins (inverted) into a larger roasting tin.

Pour the liquid from the tins over the loaves, chop some more shallots and tomatoes and mushrooms and place around the loaves, then return to the oven to continue cooking till done.

The tops will become crusty, so keep basting them.

When cooked, since they have been moulded to the loaf tin shape, they cut into very even slices very easily.

The loaves may also be used, sliced cold with salad, as an appetising summer dish.

If you intend serving them cold, then you should consider adding a couple of shelled hardboiled eggs in the centre of the mixture.

This looks very attractive when sliced, and it remains a very economical dish.

This recipe may be adapted for vegetarians by using a meat-free mince alternative and following the steps above.

SHEPHERD'S PIE

> 2lb meat base - made as for bolognaise sauce.
> (see recipe for *Booba's Meat Strudel*, page 40)
> 6 large potatoes, peeled and cut into cubes

Boil the potatoes, then mash them. Add salt and pepper

Spread the minced meat base over the bottom of a large oven dish.

Cover with the mashed potatoes, smooth over and score with fork.

Drizzle with a little lite oil.

Bake in moderately hot oven until browned and crispy.

> Serve with stir-fry cabbage, and baked beans.

GRANDMA STEAK

(as in Nana Phillips, Nana Passman, Booba et al)

2-3 lb lean chuck steak, sliced.
2 large onions, sliced
3 carrots, sliced
salt and pepper
drizzle of oil for browning onions

Season the meat well. Set aside while browning the onions in a deep lidded pan. Once onions have become transparent and started to soften, add the sliced carrots, season again well, and then lay the slices of steak on top. Cover with boiling water, taste for seasoning and cover with lid. Now, simmer very slowly for hours and hours, checking regularly to ensure that the liquid doesn't boil away. You will need gradually to add more water at intervals, and, if necessary, adjust the seasonings.

The result eventually will be steak which is as soft as butter, very dark thick sauce, and served with either mashed potatoes or (be decadent) chips!

Note that this dish is always better the following day once the flavours have had time to permeate.

Booba's
MEAT STRUDEL

1lb minced beef
3 shallots
3 tomatoes
1 clove garlic
dried or mixed chopped fresh herbs
salt and pepper
yomato puree
seasonings
1 carrot, chopped
1 stick of celery, chopped
shortcrust pastry
(frozen Snowcrest pastry is fine if fresh isn't available)

Sauté the onions, tomatoes and other vegetables, then add the chopped garlic to the pan with a drizzle of olive oil.

Cover and cook gently till softening.

Add the minced meat, stir well, season and add the tomato puree and, if necessary, a little beef stock.

Cover and cook slowly, until all is soft and resembling a Bolognaise sauce.

Roll the pastry on a cool surface and spread the cooled meat mixture leaving about 1" border. Brush the edges with egg white and gently roll up pastry to resemble a strudel.

Make sure the edges are sealed and lift carefully onto a greased or non-stick oven baking tray. Lightly mark with a sharp knife some lines where you can cut slices once it is cooked. Brush the entire strudel with beaten egg to glaze and lightly prick with a fork.

As an alternative to beef mince, use either chicken or turkey mince. In these instances it is enhanced by marinating in red wine.

Once cooked it is difficult to distinguish between poultry and red meat.

These are yummy served with crunchy roast parsnips, and *French Beans Provencale* (see page 61).

A further option is the veggie strudel

Use veggie mince, again marinated in red wine, and prepared in exactly the same way. However, the veggie mince does not need as long to cook as the meat ones.

STUFFED CABBAGE LEAVES

12 large cabbage leaves
1-2 lb minced beef or chicken
6 tablespoons rice
1 onion, chopped
1 egg
salt and pepper
1 cup chicken stock
sun-dried tomato paste.

Mix the minced meat with the beaten egg, onions and seasonings. Boil the rice till just beginning to get soft. Strain and add to the meat mixture.

Dip the washed cabbage leaves in boiling water to make them more pliable.

Shape the meat into balls and carefully wrap each ball with a cabbage leaf, ensuring the edges are well sealed. If necessary secure them with a cocktail stick. Place gently in a casserole.

Blend the sun dried tomato paste with the chicken stock and pour over the stuffed cabbage leaves. Cover and bake in oven Regulo 180c for approximately 45 minutes.

VIENNA & MASH BAKE

1 packet of cocktail viennas or frankfurters
6 shallots
1 garlic clove
4 large potatoes
seasoning

Boil viennas/frankfurters till cooked.

Chop into bite size chunks.

Sauté the onions and garlic till they become transparent.

Boil strain and mash the potatoes. In a large bowl mix all the ingredients together and spread them into a greased open oven dish.

Bake in moderately hot oven at 200c, until the potatoes become golden brown and crispy.

The ideal accompaniment to this very quick economical dish would be baked beans in tomato sauce.

Di's
QUICK SALMON TERRINE

---

3 slices of cold salmon
1lb baby new potatoes (or other salad type)
spring onions
fresh chives
fresh parsley, chopped
1 can petit pois, drained (or frozen)
1 red pepper, chopped
1 green pepper, chopped
1 hardboiled egg, chopped
pinch of salt, pepper, to taste
low fat mayonnaise
balsamic vinegar

Flake the fish

Boil potatoes, strain, cool and chop. Then, chop the spring onions, parsley and chives.

Place all main ingredients in a large bowl, mix thoroughly and season to taste.

Gradually bind together with the mayonnaise and a sprinkle of the balsamic vinegar.

Line a fish-shaped mould with cling film overlapping the sides.

Press the mixture into the mould, spreading evenly.

Once the mould is full bring over the cling film from the sides and cover very firmly. Wrap the entire mould with more cling film.

Place in the fridge and chill.

Just before eating, unwrap the film, and invert the mould onto a large platter, peel off the film wrap.

Garnish with wafer thin slices of cucumber giving the appearance of fish scales and sprinkle finely chopped parsley around the edge of the platter.

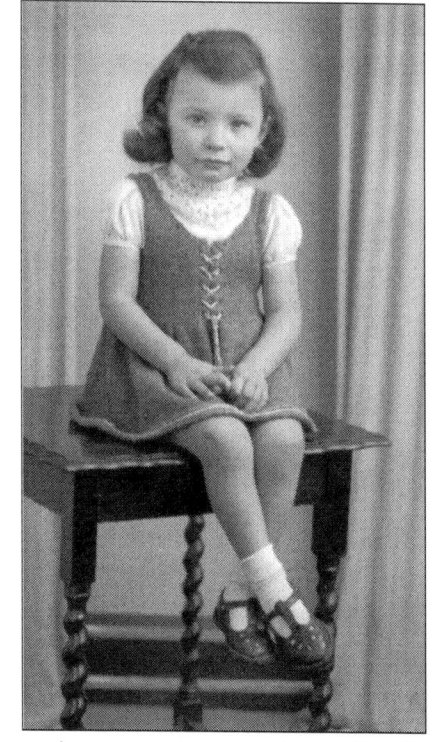

Serve and enjoy!

Chicken or meat can be substituted for salmon, in which case you should use a brioche mould instead of fish shaped container.

Loretta's
ALMOND CRUST SALMON

> 4 large salmon fillets
> salt/pepper
> approx 3-4 teaspoons mayonnaise
> 4 level teaspoons breadcrumbs
> 2 teaspoons flaked almonds
> 4 teaspoons grated low fat cheddar cheese
> 1oz melted margarine

Wash the salmon fillets. Then lightly season each piece.

Arrange in lightly oiled grill-proof dish, and spread the top of each fillet with mayonnaise.

Mix the breadcrumbs, cheese and almonds, and add melted margarine, then spread on top of each fillet, covering them completely.

Bake No7 /180c for 15-20 minutes or grill for 7 minutes.

COD WITH SPICED ONION CRUST

> 4 fillets cod
> 1 jar spiced red onion chutney
> olive oil
> spring onions
> lime juice
> 1 teaspoon caster sugar
> cayenne pepper
> 200 ml greek yoghurt (lite)
> 1 teaspoon chopped mint
> 1 clove garlic, crushed

Heat the oven to 180c. Place the fillets, skin-side down, in an oiled dish. Spread one teaspoon of chutney on top of each fillet to form a crust. Season with salt and drizzle oil on top. Bake for 15-20 minutes or till cooked through.

Trim spring onions and cut into strips, marinate in lime juice and sugar and cayenne. Toss and set aside. Mix yoghurt with garlic, mint and sea salt.

Serve each fillet with yoghurt on top and pile the onion strips on top as garnish.

Use remaining lime juice and add to the other left-over juices and pour over as a sauce.

Bibby's
FISH PIE

> 1 fillet cod/haddock
> 1 fillet smoked haddock
> 1-2 fillets salmon
> 3 leeks
> 1 cup of milk /soya milk
> chopped parsley
> 3-4 large potatoes
> 1 can condensed mushroom soup
> (or homemade mushroom sauce)
> ½ cup frozen peas.
> Salt and pepper
> dried herbs for fish
> parmesan, grated

Slice the leeks and soften in the microwave.

Gently poach the fish in a little milk. Remove from the dish, strain liquid and put to one side. Flake the fish into a bowl, add half of the chopped parsley, seasonings and herbs and mushroom soup/sauce.

Mix well.

Boil the potatoes, then mash them with a little of the fish stock/milk for added flavour, and add the remainder of the chopped parsley.

Using either individual dishes or one large one, place the fish mixture in the bottom of the dish, add the softened leeks, and cover with the mashed potatoes.

Sprinkle a little parmesan cheese over the top and bake in moderate oven at 190c.

An alternative topping is instead of mashing the potatoes they can be sliced finely and layered over the fish.

This is particularly attractive when serving as individual fish pies.

Serves approximately 6.

A salad of tossed mixed leaves makes a good accompaniment to this dish.

Hélène's
QUICK FISH PIE

Potatoes, for mashing
onions
tuna, tinned
2 eggs, lightly beaten
grated cheese, ideally cheddar
olive oil

Boil and mash the potatoes – adding olive oil to taste.

Chop the onions. Then, add the onions, tuna, eggs and grated cheese to the potatoes and mix well.

Put in an oven dish and sprinkle with a bit more grated cheese. Bake until golden, stand, serve and enjoy.

This is a great larder-raider standby, and makes a quick and easy last minute winter warmer. No hard and fast rules for quantities, it all depends on what you have in the cupboard and how many people at the table.

Helen's
MARINATED SALMON

> 1 large salmon fillet (approx 2 ½ lb)
> 1 large onion, sliced
> 1 cup white wine vinegar
> ½ - ¾ cup tomato ketchup
> 3 cloves garlic
> salt and pepper
> 3 teaspoons pickling spices
> ⅓ cup sugar

Lay half the onions in base of dish, place the fish on top. Mix all remaining ingredients together, pour over the fish.

Cover with pierced cling film and cook in microwave for 10-12 minutes. Remove from microwave and allow to cool.

Keep in the fridge for up to 2 or 3 days

May be frozen.

> This dish is ideal presented as a starter on bed of assorted salad leaves. When sliced, it can also be served as a main course.

ORGASMIC FISH DISH

1kg potatoes
4 white fish fillets, (sea bass, halibut, sole etc)
2 large onions (mild ones)
2 large tomatoes
herbs (eg: thyme, fennel anise, dill etc), to taste
salt & pepper.
bay leaf (optional)
chopped garlic

Drizzle a small amount of olive oil into a large roasting dish, preferably about 2" deep.

Season well, then peel and slice very thinly the potatoes, onions and tomatoes and spread the slices in layers across the bottom of the tin, seasoning well between each layer.

Drizzle more olive oil across the top and cover very well with tin foil. Secure the foil tightly so that all the flavours will remain contained.

Bake on the lowest setting for anything up to 8 hours, checking occasionally to ensure the vegetables do not dry out.

If necessary, either add a small amount of liquid (white wine/water) or possibly more olive oil. Olive oil flavoured with chopped garlic is ideal.

About half hour before you want to dine, place 4 seasoned fish fillets into the centre of the mixture, covering them lightly with some of the potato mixture, return them to the oven for approximately 20-30 minutes.

The taste should be "orgasmic!!!"

Nana Passman's
POACHED FISH IN EGG & LEMON SAUCE

4 fish fillets (salmon, halibut or similar)
3 shallots
2 carrots
salt and pepper

Wash and dry the fish. Season each fillet.

Slice the onions and carrots, then place all ingredients in an oven dish.

Pour over enough hot water to almost cover the fish

Cover and bake in a moderate oven until the salmon is cooked through.

The Sauce

---
6 egg yolks
juice of three lemons
sugar (or fruit sugar)

Remove fish fillets from liquid, set them out in a serving dish and leave to cool.

Strain the liquid, put into saucepan on low heat, gradually bring to almost boiling point.

Whisk egg yolks till thick and smooth, slowly add the lemon juice to the yolks, whisking continuously. Add some sugar or sweetener to taste. Pour a little of the hot liquor onto the egg and lemon mixture still beating continuously. This beating will prevent the mixture from curdling.

Once the liquid has been absorbed thoroughly, return all of it to the saucepan and the heat still stirring continuously to prevent any lumps forming.

Once this has thickened sufficiently, remove from heat, allow to cool slightly, then spoon gently over the fish. Keep the remaining sauce in a jug to be added at the table if needed.

The sauce is particularly good when served chilled.

Serve with parsley new potatoes and peas. It is also good accompanied by a green salad tossed in a light semi sweet dressing.

SALMON EN CROUTE
COULIBIAC

> puff or savoury shortcrust pastry
> (frozen, vegetarian or home-made)
> 3 salmon fillets, with squeeze of lemon juice
> (canned tuna is a cheaper substitute for salmon)
> 1 hardboiled egg, chopped
> fresh parsley, chopped
> 1 can condensed mushroom soup
> 1 cup cooked rice.
> small packet fresh spinach
> beaten egg

Gently poach the fish, cool and flake, Steam the spinach, drain well.

Roll out pastry leaving approximately 1" border.

Spread the spinach leaves over the pastry base, add the flaked fish to the condensed mushroom soup, chopped parsley, and hardboiled egg.

Mix thoroughly, then spread over the spinach. Season well.

Moisten the edges of the pastry with water, then roll gently and seal properly.

A more attractive way of preparing this dish is to cut a large fish shape out of the pastry, repeat the filling process as above; then, gently place a second slightly larger fish shaped layer of pastry over the filling and seal as above, pinching the edges together; with a sharp knife score scale shapes along the top and also add fins, place an olive where the 'eye' would be.

Lift carefully and place on a well-oiled non-stick baking tray.

Brush the entire 'fish' with beaten egg.

Bake in moderate oven approximately 200c till golden brown.

Remove from oven, cool and serve garnished on platter.

SALMON & TOMATO BAKE

1 salmon/salmon trout, filleted
3 large beef tomatoes, sliced
3 leeks, sliced
olive oil
seasonings
garlic
thyme or mixed herbs
parsley
capers
anchovies
dried chillies, chopped

Wash and dry the salmon fillets, then season well on the inner sides.

Drizzle olive oil onto a large oven dish, spread the sliced tomatoes, leeks and chopped garlic into the base of the dish.

Season well, add herbs.

Add a little water or white wine.

Chop the parsley, remaining garlic, caper and anchovies and spread this mixture onto one of the fillets.

Place the second seasoned fillet on top and gently lay the fish on the top of the tomatoes.

Drizzle a little more of the olive oil over the fish and sprinkle with some chopped dried chillies.

Bake in moderate oven for approximately 35 minutes until fish is cooked and the base mixture of tomatoes have softened.

Serve with boiled new parsley potatoes and mixed green salad tossed in semi-sweet vinaigrette.

Laurence's
COD CHEAT

> 3 – 6 frozen cod (or similar white fish) portions
> *(must be frozen, the recipe will NOT work with fresh fish)*
> one tub crème fraiche (low fat if preferred)
> 2-4 tablespoons French mustard
> pinch of chutzpah

Possibly the quickest main course ever invented, and certainly the one involving least effort and washing up.

Place the cod fillets in Pyrex oven dish.

Open the tub of crème fraiche and spoon in French mustard. Stir well then spread the cream mixture over the cod until all the fish portions are completely covered.

Place in a preheated (180-200c) oven and cook for around 40 minutes. Time varies according to thickness of fillets and water content. As the fish defrosts the water becomes a rich flavoured stock which gently blends with, and dilutes, the mustard and cream mixture.

Check, with a fork, that the white fish is cooked through, and then serve. Green vegetables and/or plain boiled or jacket potatoes are ideal partners.

FRENCH BEANS PROVENCALE

> fresh French beans
> 3 shallots
> 1 clove garlic
> large pinch of dried mixed herbs
> 1 sprig fresh rosemary
> 4 sun-dried tomatoes, chopped
> 2 teaspoons sun-dried tomato paste.
> salt and pepper

Wash, top and tail the beans, place in a shallow oven dish and cover with water. Cook in the microwave for approximately 3-4 minutes.

Chop the shallots, garlic and sun dried tomatoes. Mix together in a bowl with the mixed herbs, sun dried tomato paste, salt and pepper and a drizzle of olive oil.

Remove the beans from the microwave, strain and replace in the oven dish. Spread the mixture over them, add the sprigs of fresh rosemary, if necessary, a further drizzle of olive oil, cover with tin foil and bake in the oven for approximately 15-20 minutes. Remove the tin foil and serve.

> If you have any 'left-overs', these are particularly good when added to a tossed mixed salad.

BRAISED FENNEL

> 3-4 heads of fennel
> 6 shallots, chopped
> 2 garlic cloves, chopped
> mixed dried Italian herbs

Trim and quarter the fennel heads (If very large cut into eighths).

Put all the vegetables into an oven dish add the mixed herbs, then drizzle with a little olive oil.

Add a dash of tomato ketchup. Mix well.

Cover with lid or foil and cook till fennel is soft, at 190c.

> This dish freezes well.

Ronald's
EGGS & ONIONS

> 2 medium or 1 large Spanish onion
> 5 large eggs
> splash of milk
> butter or low-fat spread
> salt, pepper and seasoning to taste

Finely slice the onion. Heat a large frying pan and melt either butter or a low fat equivalent. When sizzling hot, add onions and fry until brown. Season well with salt and pepper. Use Aromat instead of salt if preferred.

Beat the eggs well, adding a dash of salt and a little milk. Then pour over onions when ready. Stir gently to prevent sticking and serve just before the mix is about to set.

Suggest either a milk loaf or matzo crackers to complement the dish.

Since Di married Ronald in 1958, the kitchen has been very much her domain. But whenever Ronald is given free rein, his contribution to the family fare is ever this stalwart weekend comfort grub – Fried Eggs & Onions.

MUSHROOM & ASPARAGUS QUICHE

> 8oz open-capped mushrooms
> Bunch fine asparagus spears
> fresh herbs
> 8" flan tin
> 3 eggs
> 4 fluid oz milk (or soya)
> salt and pepper
> frozen or fresh savoury short crust pastry.
> chopped parsley
> oil, or low fat alternative, for sautéing
> a few drops of balsamic vinegar

Wash, dry and trim the asparagus spears to approximately 3-4 inches (8-10cm).

Roll out the pastry and line the flan tin.

Set aside in fridge while preparing the filling.

Wipe and slice the mushrooms, heat the fat in a saucepan and sauté the mushrooms with the chopped parsley till all the juice has evaporated and they are fairly dry and browned.

Add the Balsamic vinegar and return to the heat till the vinegar has been totally absorbed.

Beat the eggs well, add the milk and seasoning.

Spread the mushrooms over the base of the flan case, pour over the beaten egg mixture, and sprinkle with mixed herbs.

Gently arrange the asparagus spears across the top.

Bake in oven at 190c until the filling has set and is a golden brown.

> For the tastiest option, serve the quiche warm rather than hot, accompanied by tossed mixed salad leaves.

ROASTED VEGETABLES PROVENCALE

3 courgettes
1 aubergine
2 red peppers
1 green pepper
bunch shallots
2 cloves garlic
sun-dried tomatoes
vine tomatoes
mixed herbs
sprig of rosemary

Chop all vegetables, lightly oil a roasting tin and spread the vegetables evenly.

Add seasonings, herbs and if using sun-dried tomatoes in seasoned oil, use some of the oil to finally toss the vegetables before placing in the oven.

Cook on a moderate heat at 190-200c, turning the vegetables regularly.

This dish is particularly good with chicken or fish dishes.

Phyllis Friedman's
CHEESE KUGEL

12oz pack egg noodles
4 tablespoons margarine
4 eggs, beaten
1 cup lite sour cream
3 tablespoons lite cream cheese
1 large can crushed pineapple, drained
⅓ cup sugar (if necessary)

Cook noodles as directed on packet.

Melt margarine in 9 x 12 Pyrex dish

Add noodles to dish and mix to coat them.

Transfer to large mixing bowl and add the eggs, soured cream and the rest of the ingredients. Mix together thoroughly, before pouring into the Pyrex dish.

Bake at 350 for 45 minutes.

SHALLOT TART
WITH
GOAT'S CHEESE

---

2 crottins de chevre (or similar goats cheese)
200ml olive oil
3 garlic cloves
1 sprig of thyme
1 sprig rosemary
200mg puff pastry
1kg shallots
400 ml parve or vegetarian stock
basil oil
50ml balsamic vinegar
salt/pepper

Cut cheese in half and place in olive oil with garlic, rosemary and thyme.

Marinate for at least 4 hours or overnight. Remove and dry.

Heat little oil from the cheese in double bottomed pan and place the shallots inside.

The shallots should just cover the bottom of the pan - there should not be any space, neither should they be on top of one another.

Fry until coloured on both sides and pour away the oil, then add the parve (or vegetarian) stock.

Simmer on the hob until the juice has reduced, then cover and place in oven.

Braise until they are well cooked at 160 degrees for approximately 45 minutes.

Remove and divide the shallots into 10 cm wide non stick moulds.

Roll out puff pastry til around 1- 2mm thick and cut 10cm discs.

Place on top of shallots and bake in the oven at 200 degrees until the pastry is golden brown approximately 20 minutes

Turn out onto plate

Grill the goats cheese until slightly browned and hot and place on top of each tart.

Drizzle a little basil oil and the balsamic vinegar around the dish. And serve.

SHAKSHUKA

> 2 red onions or 6 shallots
> 1 courgette
> 1 aubergine
> 1 fresh pepper (red, green or yellow or bits of all three)
> small jar of sun-dried tomatoes
> fresh herbs
> salt and pepper
> "Light Touch" (*non parve*) or olive oil
> 3-4 eggs

Wash, chop the vegetables and grease a deep frying pan with the fat-free Light Touch or olive oil. Gently add all the vegetables, cover and cook gently till tender.

Remove the cover and gently make three or four spaces in the pan. Now, drop an egg into each well. The whites of the eggs will gradually spread over the vegetables and then you should replace the cover and cook slowly. Once the eggs are thoroughly cooked the dish is ready to be served.

Freshly baked bagels or warmed pitta bread compliment this dish.

> If there are any 'left-overs' they can be fridged and sliced to eat cold with salad.

'LEFT-OVER' CHICKEN SALAD

---

left-over chicken
cos lettuce
chicory
cucumber
spring onions/shallots
vine tomatoes
parsley
mayonnaise
balsamic vinegar
Any other salad type veg you have left in the fridge, including cold cooked potatoes or sun-dried tomato.

Shred the chicken, wash the salad and chop finely, put all ingredients in large salad bowl. For extra flavour, add a couple of chopped sun-dried tomatoes, salt and pepper.

Mix well; add large spoonful of mayonnaise and a small amount of good Balsamic vinegar. Mix again, chill and serve. This is a very good last minute 'standby' dish and can be used for unexpected visitors.

A different version of the same salad can be made using left-over cooked salmon or white fish. If using fish, a few cubes of low fat Feta cheese can be added, and perhaps some chopped canned anchovies in olive oil, when some of the drained oil can be added to the salad dressing.

Zipporah's
YUMMY SALAD DRESSING

⅓ cup olive oil
¼ cup sugar
¼ cup lemon juice
¼ cup ketchup
2 cloves garlic, minced
½ teaspoon salt
¼ teaspoon dry mustard
¼ teaspoon paprika

Shake it up and enjoy!

When we were first invited to Shabbos supper with Rabbi Sufrin and his wife Zipporah, this delicious salad dressing was the talk of the table.

Desserts

Bibby's
GERFIKLETES COOKIES

shortcrust pastry
(frozen, vegetarian, or home made)
marmalade,
mixed dried fruits, raisins, peel, etc
(fruit cake mix is ideal)
cinnamon
ground almonds
beaten egg

Roll out the pastry on floured surface, Leave approximately ½-1 inch border, then spread with marmalade, evenly sprinkle the dried fruits and ground almonds, add generous shake cinnamon.

Moisten the edges with water. Gently roll the pastry keeping the filling from spilling out. Press the edges firmly, lift carefully and place on a greased oven tray. Make slight indents with sharp knife every 2 inches, and then brush the whole strip with the beaten egg.

Sprinkle with caster sugar and bake in moderate oven 200c, till golden brown.

Remove from oven, cut into the slices where previously marked and separate pieces. Leave to cool on wire tray.

Can be kept in airtight tin for up to 4 days, though they also freeze very well, and defrost quickly.

Booba's
HONEY CAKE

1 cup caster sugar
1 cup boiling water
1 cup oil
1lb golden syrup
1 teaspoon mixed spice
1 teaspoon cinnamon
1 teaspoon ground ginger
3 beaten eggs
1lb self-raising flour
2-3 tablespoons marmalade (chunky)

Mix all dry ingredients, then add the eggs, syrup, oil water marmalade.

Oil and line the baking tins with greaseproof paper or cake liners.

Bake at no 3 or 170c for 1¾ - 2¼ hours.

Allow to rest in the tin for a few minutes, then turn onto wire rack and cool thoroughly.

This cake freezes very well, and is essential eating for New Year and breaking the Yom Kippur fast.

CARROT CAKE

1¼ cups flour
2 teaspoons baking powder
1 tablespoon yeast
½ teaspoon cinnamon
pinch salt
¾ cup oil
walnuts for garnish
1 cup brown sugar
2 eggs
1 cup finely grated carrots

Preheat oven to 350c.

Mix together flour, baking powder, yeast, cinnamon and salt.

Blend the oil and sugar and mix well. Add eggs one at a time beating thoroughly.

Gradually add dry ingredients. Add carrots, blending well together.

Pour into greased 9 inch loaf tin.

Bake for 35-45 minutes or until the top springs back to the touch, and the edges begin to pull away from the side of the tin.

The Topping

> 2 tablespoons soft margarine
> 3oz cream cheese/low fat or crème fraiche
> 2-3 tablespoons honey, to taste
> ½ teaspoon vanilla essence
> ¼ cup wheat germ
> ¼ cup powdered milk or creamer
> ¾ cup chopped walnuts

Blend margarine and cheese or other till smooth, add honey and vanilla.

Stir in the wheat germ and powdered milk or creamer.

If the frosting is too thick, add more honey.

Spread onto the cooled cake and add walnuts to decorated.

Yvonne's
CHOCOLATE CAKE

5 eggs
11 oz margarine
1 lb sugar
7½ oz plain flour
2 tablespoons baking powder
4 tablespoons cocoa
1 teaspoon Nescafé
6 tablespoons water

In a saucepan: melt margarine, add cocoa, sugar and water, Nescafé, stir till boils cool and add egg yolks, put aside ½ cup of the mixture to keep for the topping, then add flour and baking powder.

Fold in whipped egg whites.

Bake in greased cake tin No 5 for 45 minutes.

The Topping

Retained ½ cup of mixture before adding flour etc.
(or alternatively a quarter glass of water)
1 glass sugar
2 tablespoons cocoa
2 oz margarine

Mix retained cake mixture (or water) with sugar and cocoa, and cook gently. Then add 2oz margarine and spread evenly over top of cooked cooled cake. Needs to be spread very quickly.

PESACH CINNAMON BALLS

> 4oz ground almonds
> 5 oz caster sugar
> 2 heaped teaspoon cinnamon
> whites of 2 eggs
> icing sugar, to roll

Beat egg whites until stiff peaks, then gradually add the sugar, cinnamon and almonds.

Mix well.

Roll into small balls and bake on greased tray in slow oven Gas mark 3 for approximately 20-25 minutes.

Remove from tray cool and roll in icing sugar.

Store in airtight tin.

These may also be rolled in cocoa powder instead of icing sugar.

Bibby's
BOOZY TRIFLE

> 2 jam sponge rolls or trifle sponges
> frozen soft fruits
> booze
> (Sherry, Grand Marnier, Cointreau or whatever is your tipple)
> 1 pint custard
> small carton of soya cream
> (or fresh single cream)
> fresh soft fruits
> (for garnish)

Slice the jam sponge rolls or if using trifle sponges, cut them in half and spread with any red jam.

Place the sponge slices in the bottom of a large glass dish, making sure there are no gaps.

Pour a generous amount of the booze over the sponges and press gently with a wooden spatula so that all the liquid is absorbed.

Defrost the frozen soft fruits, and gently heat in a saucepan adding any sweetener if necessary.

Add the fruits to the bowl.

Make up approximately one pint of custard using either fresh or soya milk.

Once the custard is the right consistency, stir in the carton of soya or fresh cream.

Allow the custard to cool slightly;

If you cover the custard with a damp tea towel, this will prevent a skin forming.

Once cooled, spoon it very carefully over the fruit base.

You have to be very careful that the juices from the fruit do not seep through.

This can be placed in the fridge after it has cooled completely and sealed with cling film.

Just before serving the trifle can be decorated in various ways with fresh soft fruits.

A nice touch is a few sprigs of red or blackcurrants and a couple of mint leaves.

FRUIT CAKE

> 12oz self-raising flour
> 6 oz caster sugar
> 18oz Mixed rich dried fruit
> 3 beaten eggs
> 6oz soft margarine
> 3/8 pint milk
> mixed spice
> pinch nutmeg
> booze *(optional)*

Mix together the flour and dry ingredients. Then, stir in the beaten eggs, margarine and the milk/booze.

Blend all together, or in electric mixer on slow speed.

Turn into cake tin and bake in a slow oven at 170 (gas 3-4) for approximately 2 hours.

Turn out onto wire cooling tray.

> Once cold, the cake may be kept in an airtight container for up to 2 weeks (if it lasts that long!)

LINZI TORTE

> 5oz soft margarine
> 5 oz self raising flour
> 5oz caster sugar
> 5oz ground almonds
> black cherry jam (or similar)
> 1 egg

Mix all ingredients (except the jam) together well, till they almost form a ball.

Press two-thirds of the mixture into a loose bottom lined 8-inch cake tin), then spread jam liberally over this mixture.

With remaining mixture, flour hands well and roll into rough strips, then lay crisscrossed over the jam base.

Bake in oven at regulo 3 for approximately 1 hour.

Cool in the tin for few minutes before lifting out.

Best if stored in airtight tin for a couple of days before eating.

Sprinkle liberally with icing sugar before serving.

Janet's
APPLE CAKE

8oz margarine
8oz caster sugar
2teaspoons baking powder
8oz self-raising flour
3 eggs
vanilla essence
2lb cooking apples, sliced
booze

Cream sugar and fat till white and fluffy, add yolks, flour essence etc. Beat till smooth.

Whisk whites till stiff, fold into mixture.

Pour into greased 7-8 inch loose bottom tin.

Peel, sliced apples, layer on top of mixture.

Dot with rest of margarine and sprinkle with caster sugar.

Bake approximately one hour in medium oven.

Stéphane's
LEMON TART

---

4 fresh eggs
220gms caster sugar /splenda
25cl lemon/lime juice (fresh or bottled)
25cl crème fraiche (lite)
1 pastry case (either puff or short crust)

Blind-bake the pastry case for 10 minutes at 180 degrees.

Put eggs, caster sugar crème fraiche and juice in a bowl, mix well, remove any froth created by the juice to obtain a clearer mixture

Add mixture to precooked pastry case, cook for further 25 minutes at 160 degrees.

When cold, sprinkle icing sugar and with blow torch quickly caramelise or place under hot grill for a few seconds.

Keep in the fridge for a couple of hours before serving.

Nana Phillips'
DUTCH BUTTER CAKE

> 10oz flour
> 8 oz soft margarine
> 5 ½ oz caster sugar
> 1 egg, separated
> chopped nuts

Mix the flour and sugar together in a bowl, rub in the margarine, gradually add the yolk and work into a dough.

Grease baking tray, spread dough thinly across the baking tray. Press lightly with fingers to get an even layer.

With a palette knife paste the egg white evenly across the top. Sprinkle with chopped nuts.

Bake in oven Gas No 2-3 Electric 150-160c for approximately 1¼ hours.

Remove from oven, score into squares with sharp knife. Loosen and cool on a wire tray.

Store in an airtight container.

Susie's
CHEESECAKE

> 1½ lb curd cheese
> 1 cup sugar (approx 6oz), to taste
> (I use icing sugar instead of caster)
> 1 tin of evaporated milk
> (which is fine - but I use a small single or double cream)
> 4 eggs
> 2 tablespoons custard powder
> sultanas, to taste
> shortcrust pastry

Separate the egg yolks and whites. Beat the whites until stiff and leave.

Mix the curd cheese together with the sugar until smooth rather, like whipped cream, and then add the yolks and other ingredients.

Finally, fold in the egg whites, and pour into a prepared loose bottomed baking tin (either square or round), lined with paper and twist pastry over the top, which should be brushed with egg white.

Bake in 180 oven for 10 minutes and then at 160 until golden brown on top.

> If you like your cheesecake a little on the sour side, you might add a squeeze of lemon juice into the creamed mixture.

POLENTA ORANGE CAKE

> 200 grams margarine
> castor sugar
> 1 orange (juice and zest)
> 2 tablespoons olive oil
> 4 large eggs
> 150 grams self raising flour
> 1 tablespoon baking powder
> 100 grams polenta (fine one)
> 100 grams seville orange marmalade

Beat the margarine and sugar till fluffy, grate zest of orange, add zest and oil, beat well, add the eggs gradually; at the same time gradually adding flour and baking powder. Fold in with the polenta, marmalade and orange juice.

Mix well, gently, perhaps also add some booze.

Pour into a 24cm cake tin and bake in a 170 degree oven for 60-70 minutes. Cover the top with foil after 40 minutes.

Cool on a rack.

> This makes a good companion to stewed fruits, particularly dried fruits.

Nana Passman's
MATZO PUDDING

> 1 packet matzo
> 2 eggs, beaten
> sugar, to taste (about 2 or 3 tablespoons)
> Small jar of marmalade
> handful mixed fruit/raisins, to taste
> 2 oz margarine
> cinnamon, to taste
> pinch salt
> flaked almonds and brown sugar
> *(to sprinkle on top)*

Break matzo and soak in hot water. Drain and press out excess water.

Put the margarine in a baking dish and place in oven (medium heat) to melt.

Now, put the drained matzo in bowl and add the rest of the ingredients (apart from almonds and sugar for topping). Mix together and pour into the baking dish taken from the oven, with its margarine now melted!)

Sprinkle on flaked almonds and brown sugar

Cook in medium oven for approximately 1 hour.

Remove from oven, allow to cool, cut and enjoy!

Betty's
FLORENTINES
that Hélène always makes!

---

1 tin condensed milk
(low fat works just as well)
shelled nuts
(whichever variety you prefer, some whole, some chopped)
glace cherries
raisins, peel etc
cooking chocolate
(to look fancy, use some milk, plain and white)

Mix the condensed milk with the nuts and fruits so that all are coated with the syrupy milk.

Line baking sheets with non-stick baking parchment. Dollop onto a tray. Since it all spreads, do space well apart.

Cook in medium oven 150 c.

Leave on tray to cool for a few minutes then lift to baking rack.

When cool, melt the chocolate, one type at a time!

Line fresh baking trays with non-stick baking parchment.

Spoon the melted chocolate onto the underside of the Florentines before pressing them lightly onto the prepared baking sheets.

The chocolate will spread evenly beneath them, making a smooth base to the Florentines.

Place in the fridge to cool before peeling from the sheets and storing.

This so easy that it feels like cheating, although it does take a long time.

This is a good treat to prepare whilst watching a favourite film on television.

Cousin Betty Mayover's recipe has been a treat at family simchas for as long as we can remember. Happily, she shared the recipe with Hélène, who continued the tradition.

SUMMER PUDDING

around 10 slices bread, thinly sliced
packet frozen soft fruits
sugar or Splenda sweetener
booze (any type)

Defrost the fruit, and place in saucepan with sugar/sweetener, liqueur and heat gently.

Hold back some of the fruit and liquid for use as a coulis.

Remove crusts from the bread slices.

Line either a loaf tin or individual ramekin dishes with cling film, leaving some overlap around the edges.

Cut the slices to the necessary shapes and place them slightly overlapping inside the containers.

Gradually pour the fruit onto the bread and cover with further slices of bread.

Bring the overlapping cling film over the top and secure firmly.

You may need to add further cling film.

Place dishes on a tray with heavy weights on top and fridge.

If possible leave overnight.

Just before serving unfold the cling film carefully and slide the puddings onto serving plates.

Serve with either a scoop of sorbet or ice cream and garnish with sprig of fresh mint and finely drizzle the coulis around the edge of the serving plate.

If not using ramekins to serve individual puddings, a loaf tin can be used and then the pudding may be cut into slices to serve.

Hélène's
CHOCOLATE ORANGE PEEL

> 3 large oranges
> 1 lemon
> 2 ½ cups granulated sugar (approx)
> dark chocolate

Peel the oranges and lemons, then cut the rind into strips around ¼ inch thick and length according to size of each orange or lemon.

Put in heavy based pan with about a cup of granulated sugar and water to cover.

Now, heat slowly until sugar dissolves then simmer for about 20 minutes.

Pour away the syrup and repeat the process with another 1½ cups of sugar and water. This removes the bitterness from the peel and creates a heavier syrup.

Allow to boil gently until the syrup just starts to caramelise, about the 'soft crack' stage. Be careful not to leave it too long or the peel will become too hard.

Remove the pieces of peel from the syrup and drain on a cooling rack.

Leave for several hours until dry.

Melt dark chocolate over a bain-marie and coat the peel by dipping in the chocolate.

Finally, lay the dipped chocolate strips out on non-stick baking parchment, then leave to harden in the fridge before removing from the tray.

> The flesh of the orange makes great juice, but Hélène says that her kids usually drink it before she get the chance.

Index

of

Recipes

INDEX

Almond Crust Salmon 46
Apple Cake 84
Asparagus & Mushroom Quiche 64
Aubergine Appetiser 23

Baked Meatloaf 36
Boozy Trifle 80
Borsht 8, 30
Braised Fennel 62
Butternut Squash & Ginger Soup 22

Cabbage Leaves 42
Cakes:
    Apple 84
    Carrot 76
    Cheesecake 87
    Chocolate 78
    Dutch Butter 86
    Fruit 82
    Honey 75
    Lemon Tart 85
    Linzi Torte 83
    Polenta & Orange 88
Caponata (*Eggplant Appetiser*) 23
Carrot Cake 76
Carrot Tzimmes 20
Cheese Cake 87
Cheese Kugel 67
Chicken Liver & Egg Bake 34
Chicken Salad 71
Chicken Soup 10
Chocolate Cake 78
Chocolate Orange Peel 94
Chopped Eggs & Onions 13

Chopped Liver 18
Cinnamon Balls 79
Cod Cheat 60
Cod with Spiced Onion Crust 47
Coulibiac 56

Dutch Butter Cake 86

Eggs & Onions, Chopped 13
Eggs & Onions, Fried 63
Eggplant Appetiser 23

Fennel 62
Fish Dishes :
    Almond Crust Salmon 46
    Cod Cheat 60
    Cod With Spiced Onion Crust 47
    Coulibiac 56
    Fish Pie 48, 50
    Marinated Salmon 51
    Orgasmic Fish Dish 52
    Poached Fish In Egg & Lemon Sauce 54
    Salmon en Croute 56
    Salmon And Tomato Bake 58
    Salmon Terrine 44
Fish Pie 48, 50
Florentines 90
French Beans Provencale 61
French Onion Soup 26
Fresh Pea & Mint Soup 14
Fried Eggs & Onions 63
Fruit Cake 82

Gazpacho 25
Gerfikletes Cookies 74
Grandma Steak 39

Honey Cake 75

Kneidlach 12
Leek, Lentil & Orange Soup 16
'Left-over' Chicken Salad 71
Lemon Tart 85
Linzi Torte 83

Marinated Salmon 51
Matzo Pudding 89
Meatloaf 36
Meat Strudel 40
Mushroom & Asparagus Quiche 64

Orgasmic Fish Dish 52

Pea & Mint Soup 14
Pea & Watercress Soup 24
Pesach Cinnamon Balls 79
Pesach Matzo Pudding 89
Poached Fish In Egg & Lemon Sauce 54
Polenta Orange Cake 88

Quiche 64
Quick Fish Pie 50
Quick Salmon Terrine 44

Roasted Vegetables Provencale 66

Salad Dressing 72
Salmon Almond Crust 46
Salmon En Croute Coulibiac 56
Salmon & Tomato Bake 58
Salmon Terrine 44
Shakshuka 70
Shallot Tart with Goats Cheese 68
Shepherds Pie 38

Soups:
- *Borsht 8, 30*
- *Butternut Squash & Ginger 22*
- *Chicken 10*
- *French Onion 26*
- *Gazpacho 25*
- *Leek, Lentil & Orange 16*
- *Pea & Mint 14*
- *Watercress & Pea 24*
- *Tomato with Rice & Basil 31*
- *Tomato with Gin 32*
- *Tzimmes 20*

Smoked Mackerel Pate 28
Stuffed Cabbage Leaves 42
Summer Pudding 92
Sweet & Sour Cabbage Borsht 30

Tomato Soup with Rice & Basil 31
Tomato Soup with Gin 32
Trifle 80
Tzimmes 20

Vegetable & Vegetarian dishes:
- *Braised Fennel 62*
- *Cheese Kugel 67*
- *Eggs & Onions, Chopped 13*
- *Eggs & Onions, Fried 63*
- *French Beans Provencale 61*
- *Mushroom & Asparagus Quiche 64*
- *Roasted Vegetables Provencale 66*
- *Shakshuka 70*
- *Shallot Tart with Goats Cheese 68*
- *Vegetarian Meatloaf 36*

Vegetarian Meatloaf 36
Vienna & Mash Bake 43

Watercress & Pea Soup 24
Yummy Salad Dressing 72

Printed in Great Britain
by Amazon